Marie Antoinette

Controversial Queen of France

Heather E. Schwartz

Publishing Credits

Dona Herweck Rice, *Editor-in-Chief*
Lee Aucoin, *Creative Director*
Torrey Maloof, *Editor*
Neri Garcia, *Senior Designer*
Stephanie Reid, *Photo Researcher*
Rachelle Cracchiolo, M.S.Ed., *Publisher*

Image Credits

Teacher Created Materials

5301 Oceanus Drive
Huntington Beach, CA 92649-1030
http://www.tcmpub.com
ISBN 978-1-4333-5012-2
© 2013 Teacher Created Materials, Inc.

Table of Contents

the empress of Austria and her family

Fairy-tale Beginning

Marie Antoinette (an-twuh-NET) was born into a world of wealth, status, and privilege. As the daughter of the Empress of Austria, she grew up in a palace. Marie Antoinette's life was happy and carefree. The young princess performed in operas and ballets with her siblings. She enjoyed playing with her dogs. There was no reason for her to think her life would ever change.

From an early age, Marie Antoinette was taught to be polite to everyone she met. She was charming, agreeable, and gracious. She was also considered very pretty. Marie Antoinette's mother knew that her daughter would make an important match in marriage one day. Plans were in the works by the time Marie Antoinette was 10 years old. She was to marry Louis XVI (LOO-ee). He was next in line to be the king of France. Their marriage would help strengthen the relationship between France and Austria.

To Marie Antoinette, this arranged marriage might have seemed like a fairy tale. When her husband became king, she would become the queen of France. In the end, however, she would pay a terrible price for this new royal title.

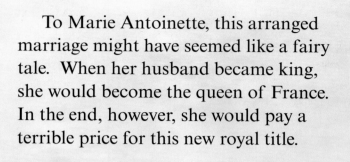

Marie Antoinette playing the piano

Austria's New Ally

In 1756, the Seven Years' War broke out in Europe, India, and North America. Several countries joined the fight for power. For the first time in history, Austria and France were **allies**. This meant that they would fight together, along with other countries, to defeat Prussia, Hanover, and Great Britain.

Political Union

Marie Antoinette's marriage to Louis XVI was not a love match. It was a political union. It helped maintain goodwill between Austria and France after the Seven Years' War ended in 1763.

Becoming the Queen of France

A New Life

The marriage between Marie Antoinette and Louis XVI had already been arranged before the two had met. When Marie Antoinette was 14, she left Austria behind forever. She traveled to France and met Louis for the first time. Several days later, on May 16, 1770, the royal wedding took place.

The couple lived at the Palace of Versailles (ver-SAHY). Marie Antoinette was rarely alone. She had attendants to keep her company and wait on her hand and foot. She had hundreds of servants who cooked, cleaned, made her wigs, and even helped her bathe. However, Marie Antoinette had no real friends in the French court.

Marie Antoinette marries Louis XVI.

King Louis XVI

An Heir to the Throne

As husband and wife, Marie Antoinette and Louis had a duty to produce a child. This child, or **heir**, would become king upon Louis's death. The couple did not have children for the first eight years of their marriage. During that time, the people of France blamed Marie Antoinette for not producing an heir. Some people in France wanted her shipped back to Austria!

As **dauphine** (DAW-feen), or the wife of the future king, Marie Antoinette was also in a position of power. She was young, pretty, and polite. She used her charm to win over the king of France, Louis's grandfather. But Marie Antoinette was a newcomer and a foreigner. Some people did not like her. They worried that she would influence Louis's decisions when she became queen. They were concerned that the king's decisions would favor Austria over France.

Palace of Versailles

In the Spotlight

Life at the Palace of Versailles was all about **etiquette** (ET-i-kit). This meant that Marie Antoinette had to follow a specific set of rules and always display good manners. She had a strict daily routine. Her schedule included church, meals, needlework, lessons, and visits with her husband, her husband's aunts, and the king. Even though she was only a teenager, she had little time for fun.

Throughout each day, Marie Antoinette had to behave in specific ways. There were rules about how she should greet people, according to their status. There were rules about how she should give orders to her servants. Marie Antoinette's lady-in-waiting taught her what to do. Marie Antoinette nicknamed her "Madame Etiquette."

Etiquette demanded that Marie Antoinette live a public life. She washed and dressed each day before an audience. She ate her meals before an audience, too. It was difficult for Marie Antoinette to adjust to her new life.

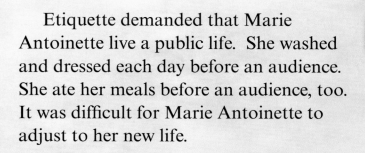
Marie Antoinette at Versailles

Royal Rebels

Marie Antoinette rebelled against etiquette in her own ways. She kept her rooms messy and stopped wearing a **corset** (KAWR-sit). She also whispered and joked with other young ladies about the strict rules.

Suspicious Minds

Being watched made Marie Antoinette uncomfortable. But she had to follow the rules. People would be offended if she did not. They would be **suspicious**, or think something was wrong, if she wanted privacy. People believed that if royalty wanted privacy, that meant there was something to hide.

Powerful Teen Queen

After King Louis XV died of smallpox in 1774, Louis XVI took the throne. That made Marie Antoinette the queen of France at age 18. When the couple first heard the news, they wept. They felt they were too young to rule France.

Marie Antoinette was popular with the French people when she first became queen. They had been unhappy with Louis XV in his later years. They were pleased to have a new royal couple in power. And, they liked Marie Antoinette because she was pretty and charming.

King Louis XV

It did not take Marie Antoinette long to begin enjoying her new role. She quickly used her power to change old customs in the French court. She stopped eating in public. She dressed in private. She also dismissed some of the attendants around her, including "Madame Etiquette."

Marie Antoinette may have felt she was making improvements. But she also made mistakes. She was disrespectful to women older than she at court. One time, she laughed during a very serious ceremony. The women at the ceremony were angry. Within a month of her reign, the French court began to turn against Marie Antoinette.

Marie Antoinette

A Country in Trouble

When Louis XVI became king, he inherited a country in trouble. France had lost the Seven Years' War and was nearly **bankrupt**. The people of France were poor and hungry. As queen, Marie Antoinette was expected to help solve these problems.

No Laughing Matter

During a **solemn** ceremony, Marie Antoinette could not stop herself from laughing at the dresses worn by the older women in the French court. News of the event traveled fast. A short song about the queen's improper laughter began to spread. "Little twenty-year-old-Queen/Since you treat people with no shame/You'll go back from where you came."

A Life of Luxury

As queen, Marie Antoinette did not think about her subjects' needs. Instead, she focused on enjoying herself and living a life of **luxury**. She liked the opera, theater, and **masquerade** (mas-kuh-REYD) **balls**. She used France's money to play games. She also spent lots of money on dresses and jewelry. Soon, Marie Antoinette was known as the Queen of Fashion.

Suffering Subjects

The peasant class in France was struggling to survive during this time. Bad weather had resulted in bad harvests. Due to the lack of crops, peasants hardly had food to eat, let alone sell. France's financial problems also caused the price of bread to rise so high that poor peasants could not afford to eat.

High Hair

Marie Antoinette wore **elaborate**, complex hairstyles that were sometimes 36 inches (91 cm) high. Her hair was decorated with flowers, jewels, fruit, feathers, and little figures. Marie Antoinette's mother told her daughter not to wear such elaborate hairstyles. She believed that a queen should have a more simplistic look. Marie Antoinette disagreed.

Marie Antoinette gets her hair done.

French peasants struggle to find food.

Marie Antoinette's new **frivolous** (FRIV-uh-luhs) lifestyle offended the large peasant class in France. These farmers and laborers no longer liked the young queen. They resented her and her thoughtless spending habits. They quickly lost hope that she would make changes that would help improve their lives.

At the Palace of Versailles, Marie Antoinette was far removed from normal life in France. Before Louis XVI and Marie Antoinette became king and queen, they had visited Paris. But the city was cleaned before their visit. Smelly mud that collected in the streets was carted away. Beggars were kept out of sight. Marie Antoinette did not know how the French people really lived. She was surprised when she later learned the French people were angry with her.

A Mother at Last

In 1778, Marie Antoinette finally gave birth to her first child, a girl. She had her first son in 1781 and her second son in 1785.

Marie Antoinette grew more mature after she had children. She settled down. She spent time with her children. They lived together at Petit Trianon (PET-ee tree-AH-no), Marie Antoinette's private retreat on the palace grounds.

Petit Trianon

Having children should have helped Marie Antoinette's reputation. She had fulfilled her duty and produced an heir. However, the people of France were still suspicious of Marie Antoinette. They did not understand her need for privacy at Petit Trianon. They said she spent too much time there when she should be at court. They continued to look for reasons to dislike her. Sometimes, people would invent rumors about Marie Antoinette to spread hatred for the queen.

Marie Antoinette may have changed. But many of her subjects were unwilling to change their minds about her. They wanted to believe the worst.

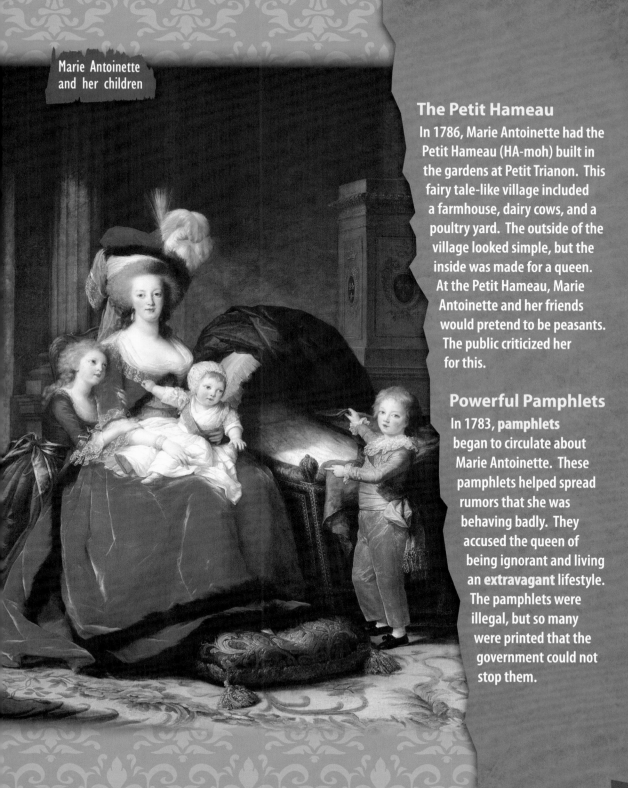

Marie Antoinette and her children

The Petit Hameau

In 1786, Marie Antoinette had the Petit Hameau (HA-moh) built in the gardens at Petit Trianon. This fairy tale-like village included a farmhouse, dairy cows, and a poultry yard. The outside of the village looked simple, but the inside was made for a queen. At the Petit Hameau, Marie Antoinette and her friends would pretend to be peasants. The public criticized her for this.

Powerful Pamphlets

In 1783, **pamphlets** began to circulate about Marie Antoinette. These pamphlets helped spread rumors that she was behaving badly. They accused the queen of being ignorant and living an **extravagant** lifestyle. The pamphlets were illegal, but so many were printed that the government could not stop them.

Affair of the Diamond Necklace

The Scam

In 1785, Marie Antoinette was caught up in a **scandal** involving a diamond necklace that was for sale in France.

The scandal began with the Comtesse (KOHM-tess) de la Motte (mott). She contacted the Cardinal de Rohan (RO-hahn). He was out of favor with Marie Antoinette. The comtesse claimed she could help the cardinal. She encouraged him to write letters to the queen. She had a friend answer the letters, signing the queen's name.

The comtesse then arranged a meeting between the cardinal and the queen. The cardinal did not know that he really met with an **impersonator**, not Marie Antoinette. After the meeting, he was convinced Marie Antoinette loved him.

Comtesse de la Motte

Cardinal de Rohan

Family Rumors

Both Marie Antoinette and her mother, Maria Theresa, greatly disliked the Cardinal de Rohan. Prior to the affair of the diamond necklace, the cardinal told Maria Theresa that her daughter was living an immoral life in France. Maria Theresa scolded the cardinal for gossiping. Maria Theresa blamed the cardinal for many of the rumors surrounding her daughter. The cardinal then wrote a letter to Marie Antoinette in which he spoke poorly of her mother. This greatly upset the queen.

Where Is the Necklace?

The diamond necklace involved in the scam was later broken into pieces. The pieces were then sold in London, England.

Next, the comtesse told the cardinal that Marie Antoinette wanted the expensive diamond necklace that was for sale. The comtesse told the cardinal to get it. She promised that the queen would pay for it later. The cardinal got the necklace and gave it to the comtesse to deliver to the queen. But the necklace never made it to the queen.

When the jewelry makers asked for payment, the scandal was discovered. Marie Antoinette played no part in the scandal, but it hurt her already poor reputation. The public did not believe that she was innocent.

the diamond necklace

Royal Scapegoat

After the affair of the diamond necklace, Marie Antoinette could no longer go to the theater and opera. Audience members hissed at her when they saw her. They applauded shows that depicted her as a cruel queen.

The queen was a more serious woman now. Her husband needed her. She started paying attention to politics. By 1787, France was nearly bankrupt. King Louis XVI could not solve the crisis. He was weak and uncertain. Marie Antoinette was not an expert on the issues. However, she was stronger and more decisive than her husband. She tried to help the king by offering suggestions.

political cartoon about the Third Estate rising up against the clergy and nobility

the French royal family

The people of France criticized her for interfering. They felt it was not a woman's place to rule. More pamphlets were printed to insult the queen and further damage her reputation. The pamphlets claimed she was trying to take over the government. Marie Antoinette had lived for many years as a Frenchwoman, but the pamphlets reminded people their queen was an Austrian foreigner.

Marie Antoinette had become a **scapegoat** (SKEYP-goht). She was blamed for all of France's problems.

The French Revolution

A Political Crisis

In May 1789, the deputies, or representatives, of the Estates-General came to Versailles. The king and queen rode out to meet them. A crowd gathered. When they saw King Louis XVI, they applauded. They greeted Marie Antoinette with silence.

Marie Antoinette was upset. But she soon had a political crisis to handle. In June, the Third Estate, made up of peasants, **defected**. It left the Estates-General and renamed itself the National Assembly. The National Assembly wanted a more **democratic** government. The queen encouraged her husband not to give in to their demands.

The king locked the National Assembly out of their meeting place. But, the National Assembly continued to meet in an unused tennis court. Members took an oath. They vowed to meet until France had a new constitution. This was known as the Tennis Court Oath.

Marie Antoinette encouraged the king to set up troops against the National Assembly. She knew they wanted to overthrow the **monarchy**. This decision angered the people. On July 14, they responded by storming the Bastille (ba-STEEL), an old prison. They wanted the weapons that were kept there. They destroyed the prison towers and killed the Bastille's governor. The French Revolution had begun.

the Tennis Court Oath

storming the Bastille

A New Charter

The National Assembly adopted a new charter in August 1789. The Declaration of the Rights of Man and the Citizen was based on the American Declaration of Independence.

Storming the Bastille

Another reason the National Assembly stormed the Bastille was the king's decision to get rid of Jacques Necker (zhahk NEK-er). Necker was the finance minister for France. He had suggested that the king listen to the National Assembly and try to work with them. Marie Antoinette did not like this idea and urged her husband to remove Necker from office. After the Bastille fell, Necker was placed back in office.

The Great Fear

After the storming of the Bastille, rumors began to spread. People believed the government might overthrow the Third Estate. They were worried the king would give orders to burn villages, destroy crops, and create widespread food shortages. The people rioted throughout France. This was known as the Great Fear.

Let Them Eat Cake?

Marie Antoinette was criticized for not sympathizing with her hungry subjects. There is a story that says that when Marie Antoinette was told her subjects had no bread, she replied, "Let them eat cake!" The story is not true, but it is still told centuries later.

Driven from Versailles

Fearing for their safety, many friends and members of the court left Versailles. But Marie Antoinette told her husband that their family should stay. She felt that fleeing would make them seem cowardly. He did not want to weaken the monarchy and agreed to stay. However, the monarchy was no longer truly in power. The National Assembly was gaining ground.

Hundreds of angry French women gathered in Paris. They wanted bread. They wanted to bring the king to Paris as a prisoner. They wanted to kill Marie Antoinette. They began marching to Versailles. They carried kitchen knives, brooms, pitchforks, and other items they could use as weapons. Along the way, thousands of soldiers joined them.

The women of Paris march to Versailles.

The royal family trapped in Versailles.

The mob reached the palace and broke in. The mob killed the bodyguards and broke into Marie Antoinette's bedroom, but she had fled just in time. The mob stabbed and tore apart her bed. When Marie Antoinette finally met the mob, she **appeased**, or calmed them, by **curtsying**. The mob took this as a sign of respect. The people's murderous mission changed. They were now determined to bring both the king and queen back to Paris as prisoners.

Maximilien Robespierre

Radical Revolutionaries

In 1790, the Jacobin (JAK-uh-bin) party began to attract more members. It was a **radical** political group. The Jacobin Party was known for its violence and democratic ideals. The leader of the party was Maximilien Robespierre maks-uh-mill-IYAN ROHBZ-pee-air). He was a key figure in the French Revolution.

Help!

King Louis XVI secretly wrote to his cousin, Charles IV, in Spain, to ask for help in fighting off the revolution. Marie Antoinette wrote to other countries, too, using invisible ink. She asked that the countries invade France and restore the monarchy.

Life as a Prisoner

During the ride to Paris, the royal family was harassed and threatened. The life they had known was over forever. But to Marie Antoinette's surprise, she and her husband were greeted warmly when they arrived in the city. Rooms at the old Tuileries (TWEE-luh-reez) Palace were **restored** for the royal family. They were allowed to have friends and servants join them there. Furniture was brought from Versailles. The people of France claimed there would be no more violence against the royal family.

Still, Marie Antoinette's family lived as prisoners in the Tuileries Palace. The queen knew that spies watched her every move. She feared for her safety and for her children's safety. She wanted to escape to the country. However, she could not leave when there was still hope that the monarchy would regain power.

While at Tuileries, Marie Antoinette acted as if life were normal. She had card parties and dined publicly. At the same time, she secretly worked against the revolution. She knew she needed help. She learned to read and write in code. She began communicating with other countries. During Marie Antoinette's lifetime, these acts of **treason** were never discovered.

The royal family is taken from Versailles to Tuileries.

Escape Attempt

Marie Antoinette felt that her life was in danger. She knew her children and husband were not safe in France anymore. In June 1791, she planned an escape to Austria. The king, queen, and their children dressed as common people for the journey. However, their extravagant coach gave them away. They were caught 40 miles (64 km) from the border. The royal family was arrested and brought back to Paris.

Later that year, France became a constitutional monarchy. Marie Antoinette was against it. However, she urged her husband to accept the new government. King Louis XVI swore to uphold the Declaration of the Rights of Man and the Citizen. That gave him back some power. From now on, he would share his rule with the National Assembly.

the arrest of the royal family

Declaration of the Rights of Man and the Citizen

Brunswick Manifesto

The Brunswick Manifesto reached Paris on July 28, 1792. It was a warning to France from the commander of the Austrian and Prussian armies. It said the French should restore the monarchy and no harm should come to the royal family. The people saw it as proof that King Louis XVI was an enemy of the revolution.

September Massacres

Between September 2 and 6, 1792, revolutionaries killed about 1,500 prisoners to prevent them from helping those against the revolution. One was Marie Antoinette's friend, the Princesse de Lamballe (LAHM-ball).

In 1792, the National Convention was elected. It ended the French monarchy for good. France was declared a republic. Louis and Marie Antoinette were now ordinary citizens. Their **reign** was officially over.

Calm Queen

By 1793, the royal family had been taken to Temple Prison. King Louis XVI was charged with treason and sentenced to death. On January 21, he was **executed** by **guillotine** (GEE-uh-teen) in front of 10,000 people. A guillotine was a machine with a heavy blade. When the blade was released, it would fall on the person's neck, chopping off his or her head.

In October 1793, Marie Antoinette was charged with treason and other crimes. The court had no proof of her treason or that she committed any crimes. Some historians say she was convicted based on her poor reputation. She, too, was sentenced to death by guillotine.

Guards chopped off Marie Antoinette's hair, bound her arms behind her back, and took her to the guillotine in an open cart. Crowds lined the streets and jeered at Marie Antoinette as she passed by. But, she remained calm and did not cry. When the guillotine's blade fell, the crowd cheered. The former queen of France was dead at the age of 37. In a letter left in her prison cell, Marie Antoinette gave all her love to her children.

Marie Antoinette is one of the most infamous women in history. She will be remembered as the controversial and last queen of France.

the execution of King Louis XVI

Marie Antoinette and her children in Temple Prison

Reign of Terror

On September 5, 1793, the Reign of Terror began. At least 300,000 enemies of the French Revolution were arrested during the next 11 months. Of those prisoners, over 17,000 were executed.

The Children's Fate

King Louis XVI and Marie Antoinette's two children remained in prison after their parents' executions. Louis Charles died in prison in 1795 at the young age of 10. His older sister was sent to Austria when she was 17 in exchange for French prisoners.

Marie Antoinette being taken to her execution

Glossary

allies—people or groups that are united for the same cause

appeased—soothed

bankrupt—lacking money to pay debts

corset—a stiff undergarment worn by women

curtsying—a form of bowing made by women

dauphine—the wife of the heir to the throne

defected—stopped supporting a cause or group

democratic—appealing to the common people

elaborate—fancy; made with effort

etiquette—rules about social behavior

executed—legally put someone to death

extravagant—beyond what is reasonable

frivolous—silly; not being serious when it is necessary

guillotine—a machine for cutting off a person's head

heir—a person who inherits a title when someone dies

impersonator—a person who is pretending to be someone else

luxury—something of great expense and comfort

masquerade balls—parties where people wear masks and fancy outfits

monarchy—a system of rule with a king or queen in power

pamphlets—short, printed, and unbound publications with no covers or with paper covers

radical—extreme

reign—a period of time when a ruler is in power

restored—returned something to better condition

scandal—an event that causes damage to a reputation

scapegoat—someone who is unfairly blamed

solemn—serious

suspicious—not trusting

treason—an act of disloyalty to one's country

Index

Your Turn!

Marie Antoinette was 14
when she left her home in
Austria and
She travele
met Louis
married hi
Marie Ant
the Palace
life was no

A Day in t

Imagine tha
Antoinette.
you describ
Remember
the situatio